1st Recital Series

PIANO ACCOMPANIMENT

FOR E♭ ALTO SAXOPHONE

Including works of:
- James Curnow
- Craig Alan
- Douglas Court
- Mike Hannickel
- Timothy Johnson
- Ann Lindsay

Solos for Beginning
through Early Intermediate
level musicians

CURNOW® MUSIC

EXCLUSIVELY DISTRIBUTED BY

HAL•LEONARD® CORPORATION

7777 W. BLUEMOUND RD. P.O. BOX 13819 MILWAUKEE, WI 53213

Edition Number: CMP 0752-02-401

1st Recital Series
Solos for Beginning through Early Intermediate level musicians
Piano Accompaniment for Alto Saxophone

ISBN: 978-90-431-1681-7

Foreword

High quality solo/recital literature that is appropriate for performers playing at the Beginner through Early Intermediate skill levels is finally here! Each of the **1st RECITAL SERIES** books is loaded with exciting and varied solo pieces that have been masterfully composed or arranged for your instrument.

Included with the solo book there is a professionally recorded CD that demonstrates each piece. Use these examples to help develop proper performance practices. There is also a recording of the accompaniment alone that can be used for performance (and rehearsal) when a live accompanist is not available. A separate solo E♭ Alto Saxophone book is available [edition nr. CMP 0686.02].

Table of Contents

1. NOCTURNE

Eb ALTO SAXOPHONE

Ann Lindsay (ASCAP)

Johannes Brahms
2. FINALE FROM SYMPHONY #1

Eb ALTO SAXOPHONE

Arr. **Timothy Johnson** (ASCAP)

Victor Herbert
Fantasy On
3. DAGGER DANCE
from "NATOMA"

Eb ALTO SAXOPHONE

Arr. **Craig Alan** (ASCAP)

4. SKATER'S WALTZ

Douglas Court (ASCAP)

Engelbert Humperdinck
5. SUITE FROM HANSEL AND GRETEL

Eb ALTO SAXOPHONE

Arr. **James Curnow** (ASCAP)

1. Evening Prayer

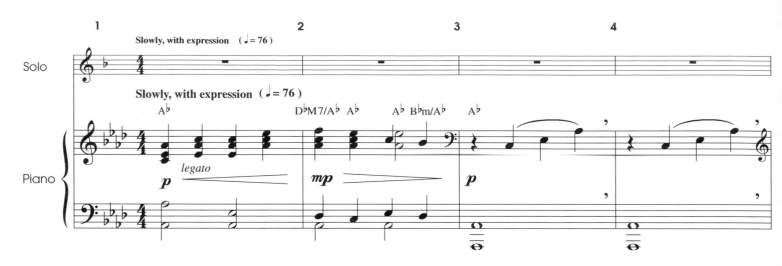

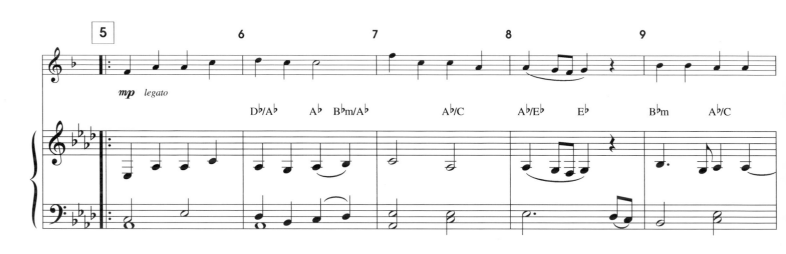

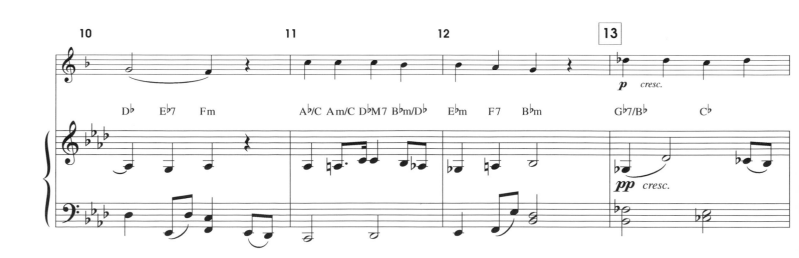

Engelbert Humperdinck

6. SUITE FROM HANSEL AND GRETEL

Eb ALTO SAXOPHONE

Arr. **James Curnow** (ASCAP)

2. A Tiny Little Man

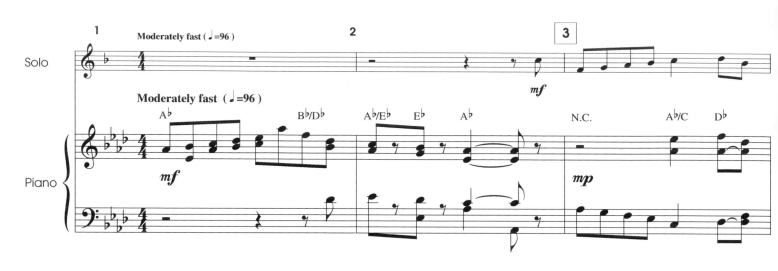

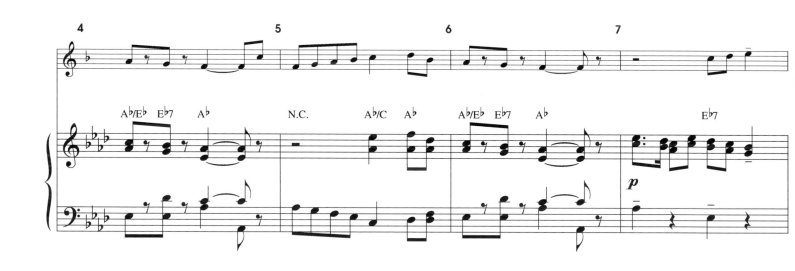

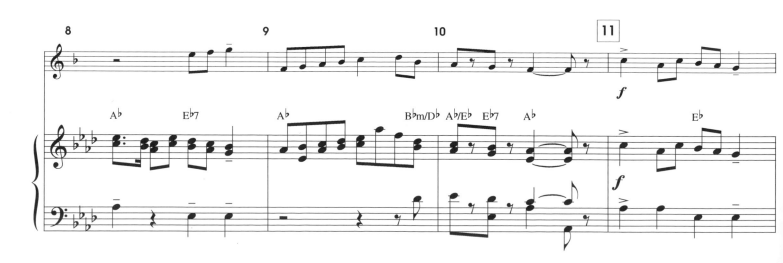

Frederic Chopin

7. FANTAISIE IMPROMPTU

E♭ ALTO SAXOPHONE

Arr. **Ann Lindsay** (ASCAP)

8. SAXOPHONE A LA CARTE

Eb ALTO SAXOPHONE

Mike Hannickel (ASCAP)

W. A. Mozart
9. ANDANTE
from LA CI DAREM LA MANO

From Don Giovanni

Eb ALTO SAXOPHONE

Arr. **Ann Lindsay** (ASCAP)

E♭ ALTO SAXOPHONE

10. A WALTZ FOR ESTHER

Mike Hannickel (ASCAP)

11. THE WATER IS WIDE

E♭ ALTO SAXOPHONE

Traditional
Arr. Craig Alan (ASCAP)

12. PANTOMIME

Eb ALTO SAXOPHONE

Arr. **James Curnow** (ASCAP)